Little Children's Bible Books

JOHN

Retold by Anne de Graaf   Illustrated by José Pérez Montero

B&H
BROADMAN
& HOLMAN
PUBLISHERS

Dedicated to
Pedro Pérez Rollán and Mariusz Szeloch

JOHN

Published in 2001 by Broadman & Holman Publishers,
Nashville, Tennessee

Text copyright © 2001 Anne de Graaf
Illustration copyright © 2001 José Pérez Montero
Design by Ben Alex
Conceived, designed and produced by Scandinavia Publishing House
Printed in Hong Kong
ISBN 0-8054-2195-5

John was a follower of Jesus. He was a fisherman. Jesus loved John very much, and John loved Jesus very much. John would follow Jesus anywhere.

7

Near the end of Jesus' life, his enemies wanted to kill him. So Jesus prayed to God. He was very sad. Then he asked a few of his followers, including John, "Stay with me and pray."

Jesus prayed as hard as he could. Pray now as hard as you can, for someone you love.

After Jesus died, one of the women who belonged to the group of Jesus' followers, burst through the door. She ran up to John.

Now you burst through the door. Then cry out what this woman told John, "Something terrible has happened! They've taken Jesus' body away! He's not in the cave anymore!"

11

John looked at Peter. The two dashed off to the garden where Jesus had been buried one, two, three days earlier. They panted and raced. John beat Peter.

Run around the room as fast as you can. One, two, three times!

At the cave, John looked inside. He saw nothing but the cloths Jesus was wrapped in. John saw and believed. Jesus had risen from the dead!

Wrap yourself up in a sheet. Now ask the person reading to unwrap you while you sing, "Jesus is risen. He is risen indeed!"

After Jesus went to heaven, John and Peter led Jesus' friends. Sometimes they went to jail, just because they healed people in the name of Jesus.

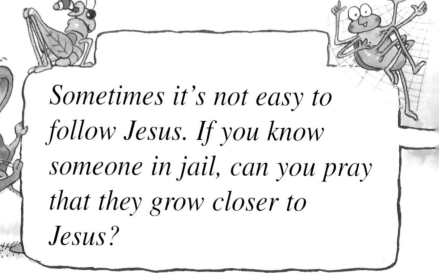

Sometimes it's not easy to follow Jesus. If you know someone in jail, can you pray that they grow closer to Jesus?

17

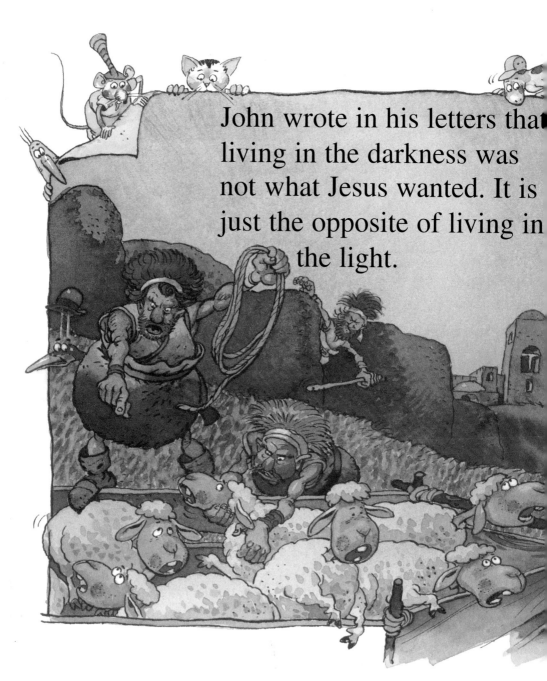

John wrote in his letters that living in the darkness was not what Jesus wanted. It is just the opposite of living in the light.

John wrote letters to Jesus' followers.
He reminded them that Jesus said,
"Love one another as I have loved you."

John called this living in the light and walking in the truth of Jesus' own love for us.

Find all the ways on these pages that you can show someone you love them.

When John was an old man, he had a special vision from God. He wrote down Jesus' words, "I'm here for anyone who asks me into their lives. I'm standing at the door, knocking, waiting for them to hear my voice and open the door."

Go to the door, close it, then have the person reading to you knock on it. Opening the door and letting them in is just like you asking Jesus into your own little heart.

John wrote that Jesus said, "Even when someone has done something wrong, if they turn to me and say they are sorry, I can help them start over again. If they do this, I will be with them forever and never leave them."

Name all the places you can think of where Jesus is with you. Name some more. Is there anywhere he ISN'T?

In John's vision, he heard music and saw a huge crowd, the followers of Jesus from all time and all countries. No one could count all the people!

31

John's glimpse of the new heaven and new earth shows what God's kingdom will be like. There will be no more bad people and no more sadness.

Name three things you think heaven will be like.

In John's vision he saw a new Jerusalem. Those who had chosen to follow Jesus were there with God, and nothing evil was there. It was a place of light and happiness.

John wrote often about light, living in the light, and God's kingdom as a place of light. Turn the light on and off now. Who is the Light of the world?

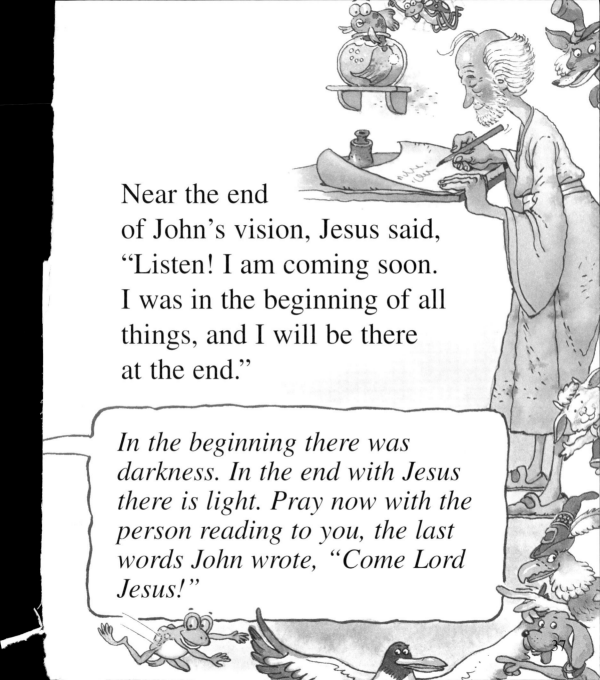

Near the end
of John's vision, Jesus said,
"Listen! I am coming soon.
I was in the beginning of all
things, and I will be there
at the end."

*In the beginning there was
darkness. In the end with Jesus
there is light. Pray now with the
person reading to you, the last
words John wrote, "Come Lord
Jesus!"*

A NOTE TO THE big PEOPLE:

The *Little Children's Bible Books* may be your child's first introduction to the Bible, God's Word. This book about John is based on passages from the Gospel according to John, the Book of Acts and John's Letters in the Bible. This is a DO book. Point things out and ask your child to find, seek, say, and discover.

Before you read these stories, pray that your child's little heart would be touched by the love of God. These stories are about planting seeds, having vision, learning right from wrong, and choosing to believe. Pray together after you read this. There's no better way for big people to learn from little people.

A little something fun is said in italics by the narrating animal to make the story come alive. In this DO book, wave, wink, hop, roar, or do any of the other things the stories suggest so this can become a fun time of growing closer.